HOW TO GET OUT OF YOUR OWN WAY

How to Get Out of Your Own Way:

The Empowerment Guide & Workbook to Get Your Mind Right

Shauntee B.

First Printing: 2020

ISBN: 978-1-7353916-8-7

Ordering Information:
Visit www.IGotMyMindRight.com
Special discounts are available on quantity purchases by corporations, associations, educators, and bulk orders.

U.S. trade bookstores/wholesalers:
Please contact Shauntee B Consulting, LLC
Email: info@ShaunteeB.com
Website: www.ShaunteeB.com

Dedication

To Kionte, Naiya, and Tyanna, my three heartbeats.
Thank you for pushing me to strive to be a better version of myself daily. You guys give me strength beyond understanding because of you all I make it a priority to get my mind right. Always remember you can do whatever you set your mind to.

Table of Contents

Acknowledgments

A special and heartfelt Thank You to my mom and friends for inspiring and motivating me... for always being a resource when people I depended upon dropped the ball. Without you all, this book would have never been completed.

The
Empowerment
Guide

Introduction

Hey Y'all Hey!

So, people often wonder how I am so positive. I'm always encouraging, not only myself but others to keep pushing, despite life sometimes feeling like an episode of a Lifetime movie. I learned through all the bullshit that one of the keys to living a better life is all about perspective and how you view the things you are experiencing. Once you master this, you will realize how much this impacts and changes your life. By the time you are finished with this book, I hope that you apply some of these techniques to your life and watch the greatness unfold. The time is NOW to get out of your own way and **GET YOUR MIND RIGHT!!!**

Chapter 1: **Optimism – The Basics**

What is Optimism?

One of the main ingredients of self-development and a primary skill is optimism. Yes, OPTIMISM...We've all heard the word but do you know what it really means and do you apply it to your daily life?

Optimism is an important part of positive psychology – "a branch of psychology that deals with how individuals can be happier." Our outlook on life is a very important part of our development as people and a critical factor that is responsible for our overall growth and success in life. Who knew...huh? But now that you know, the real question is "Are you ready to GET YOUR MIND RIGHT and apply the necessary changes?"

People with a pessimistic (negative) outlook always find it more difficult to navigate through life than those who are optimistic (positive). They may find it difficult to advance in their careers, relationships, or life in general. How we react to the failures and disappointments in our lives can shape many things. It may mean the difference between experiencing events in our lives as a loss or a lesson.

My goal is to help you better understand what optimism is all about, its origin, definition, and how you can apply it to your life daily. You will learn why it's important and how you can become a daily optimist. You'll see its many potential benefits and why maintaining an optimistic and positive outlook on life is **KEY** to your well-being, relationships, and career choices. So, grab a glass of wine or your drink of choice, get comfortable, and let's get your mind right.

You probably have that one friend who always remains in good spirits, despite experiencing adverse events and disappointments in their life, which could be annoying or overwhelming for you at times. Perhaps there were times when they faced problems that might have made them bitter, angry, or depressed. Instead of having a pity party, they always take what they can learn from the situation. They look forward to each passing day with high expectations. These people, my dear friends, are known as optimists! They always seem to find the good in any situation and anticipate only favorable things. For example, I have a friend that I vent to all the time, and no matter what the problem is or what I am complaining about, she always finds ways that a situation can work in my favor. She never lets me stay stuck in the negative.

Optimism is a mindset that we can all practice daily to enable us to cope with life's many challenges. It is a bomb ass quality to possess. Optimism comes from the Latin word Optimus, meaning "best," and translates as the inclination to believe, expect, or hope that things will ultimately turn out for good.

Studies in the field of positive psychology reveal a lot about the positive impact that being optimistic has on our mental health. Psychologists see optimism as a personality trait, meaning that it is stable to some extent and consistent over time.

There have also been reports from other research studies highlighting its many benefits to our physical health. Optimists have been proven to have a longer lifespan and they also fall sick less often than pessimists. An optimist believes that their happiness is their sole responsibility. They don't place any blame on themselves when bad events happen. If for any reason anything goes wrong for an optimist, they often see it only as a temporary setback and they brush it off and move on with their lives.

Pessimists, on the other hand, think the opposite way. They believe that their lives are out of control and expect the worst to happen. They don't expect anything good to come from their actions or their relationships with others. At worse, they think that one mistake will inevitably lead to a series of unfortunate events in the future. For example, a pessimistic person may have been through something traumatic in their lives and no longer see the good in anything. They may feel like they deserved it, play the victim, or just down on life. They never see the light at the end of the tunnel. Where on the other hand, an optimistic person has been through something traumatic but decided to turn that situation into a positive and see the good in all things.

When positive events do happen, the pessimist characterizes it as luck. They see it as a chance encounter with good luck that they do not deserve, and one that will most likely never happen again. They have given up on believing in themselves to ever be capable of producing anything good and they don't expect good from others either. We have to get out of that negative headspace, which can be draining as hell.

So we see that optimists don't see bad days as a permanent way of life, rather they see them as valuable learning experiences. For them, even when going through the most miserable days, they maintain a firm conviction that tomorrow will be better. We have to always remember that our setbacks are setting us up for our greatest comeback. They usually bear other similar positive characteristics that help relieve severe stress and depression while increasing overall happiness and promoting good health.

- They focus their thoughts on, reflect on, and emphasize the positive things in life.

- They show gratitude and appreciation for their blessings.

- They don't complain when bad events occur.

- They don't feel constrained by anything or anyone from achieving success and reaching their goals.

- They believe in abundance.

- They are confident that the world is full of equal and enough opportunities for everyone to be successful.

Why is Optimism Important?

There have been various studies in recent times on the essentials of optimism and its importance. When going through the daily struggles of life, and excuse my French, but we all know life can be a fucking struggle at times; it is easy to feel overwhelmed if we are faced with difficult days, hard times, and stressful periods. Choosing to be optimistic and positive even in the face of adversity can bring benefits to you and the people around you.

There are many reasons why living an optimistic life is the best choice. Optimism helps us persevere when things get difficult. People also enjoy being around positive and happy people. Nobody likes to be in the company of a Debbie Downer; everyone prefers hanging out with a Positive Patty. If you constantly find yourself with self-defeating thoughts in your mind, you will most likely become a victim of such thinking in the future. However, if you focus your mind on positive things, you will most certainly attract all such positivity into your life.

It is just as Henry Ford said, "Whether you think you can or you think you can't… Either way, you are right."

Here are some of the Benefits of Optimism:

1. It Promotes Good Health

People with positive thoughts usually have lower anxiety and we all know anxiety can be a bitch. Dwelling on negativity is detrimental to your health and wellbeing; it breeds disaster. Optimism will help keep your blood pressure down, provide significantly better blood sugar and cholesterol levels, afford healthier body mass indexes, and make you generally happier and less stressed...LONG STORY SHORT...THE HAPPIER YOU ARE THE HEALTHIER YOU ARE! Let Debbie Downer deal with her high blood pressure and anxiety due to her negative outlook on life.

2. It Aids in Greater Achievement and Better Performance

Optimistic people are usually self-confident, focused, highly motivated, productive, resilient in the face of adversity, and have high self-esteem. All these attributes enable them to take on greater challenges and achieve greater things in life. Teams perform better and create a more positive synergy when each member is as optimistic as the next. Pessimistic people, on the other hand, are typically constrained by their negative beliefs, which make them shy away from being innovative or trying adventurous things. It's time to fix our crowns, hold our heads up with confidence, and live life to the fullest. Let that pessimistic shit go!!

3. It Spreads Good Vibes and Makes Your Life Less Painful

Optimism is contagious, just like this damn Corona Virus pandemic. By always maintaining an upbeat attitude, others around you will be inspired to mirror you. Also, those who think positive thoughts day in and day out usually have a higher pain tolerance than those who tend to be negative. Pessimistic individuals are less likely to keep their emotions in check when they experience pain, perhaps due to their expectation of pain in life.

4. It helps you Stay Youthful

Research has also shown that optimism increases longevity, promotes healthy living, and increases your mental flexibility. Working on your mindset is the key to maintaining a youthful look. According to the results of a study conducted at University College London, there is a direct link between positive thoughts and healthy aging. Now, don't we all want to look like Denzel or Angela Bassett when we get 60 years old? We have to maintain a positive attitude and mindset.

5. It Helps You Have More Abundance in Love and Relationships

Psychologists have always acknowledged the importance of being optimistic. They point out that positive thinkers are more likely to have a better chance of love and relationships. Even though they may face the same challenges in relationships as pessimists do, optimists tend to work harder and more effectively at love and relationships because they concentrate on the good rather than the bad.

Can Optimism Be Learned?

The good news about optimism is that it is a skill that can be taught and learned. Research shows that there are various strategies that we can use to learn optimism, including cognitive behavioral therapy and by simply envisioning the best possible outcome of things in the future.

Psychologist Charles Carver introduced Cognitive Behavioral Therapy (CBT) as a means of learning optimism. With this technique, you can understand and challenge the perception that you may have about yourself, the world, and the future. On the other hand, imagining the future, which also means visualizing the best possible outcome, has its benefits.

You can also begin to learn optimism by first working on your mindset and by practicing being joyful, grateful, and happy. It is easy for a person to become pessimistic when they are passing through a series of negative events. But overcoming these ultimately depends on you and your willingness to try. It's time to manifest the bomb ass life you deserve.

Optimism is ultimately more about resilience than temperament. Most people have experienced difficulties and failures in their lives. It is the reaction to these adverse situations and what people tell themselves in their subconscious minds that matter.

When bad things happen, the optimist sees it as only temporary. They inherently believe that they have the power to turn the situation around for the better. The pessimist, on the other hand, sees the setback as permanent and believes that it will undermine everything that they have done so far and into their future. For example, we all have experienced or are currently facing financial hardship. The optimistic person knows that this is a minor setback and will work hard to become debt-free. While the pessimist person will say "woe is me" and will continue to stay in that broke mindset.

Some people describe the optimistic pattern of thinking as the 'glass half full' mentality, whereas the pessimist sees the glass as half empty.

Learning to be optimistic when faced with struggles involves consciously altering your thought processes so that you can re-wire your brain to think more positively.

Both the pessimist and the optimist experience negative events when they happen. However, rather than lingering in self-defeat and blaming themselves for the bad outcome, the optimist acknowledges the situation and looks for ways to recover from it. They do this by finding the courage to consciously change the habit of negative self-talk and self-limiting beliefs into positive self-talk and positive thinking.

Becoming more optimistic is a skill that is quite simple to learn but requires consistent effort and practice on your part. There are several ways by which you can learn optimism. One such way is through the ABCDE model as proposed by psychologist Martin Seligman, which represents Adversity, Belief, Consequence, Disputation, and Energization.

Better understand the idea behind this model of learning by studying the example given below:

A. Adversity:
When someone rushes past you, bumps into you, and knocks your drink to the ground.

B. Belief:
You exclaim (and believe), "That person deliberately bumped me and didn't even apologize." WTF???

C. Consequence:
Feelings of bitterness and anger gradually overwhelm you and continue to be with you for the rest of the day, which will make your attitude suck.

D. Disputation:
You realize that the negative feelings you are experiencing will not bring any good for you and so you decide to take a stand against it. You place yourself in the other person's shoes and begin to find reasons behind their action. Perhaps they needed to rush to the emergency room

or to rush off to another pertinent crisis. You allow yourself to forgive and forget, then move on.

E. Energization:

Upon overcoming the negative feelings you once experienced, you feel energized and happy to have successfully taken control of your thoughts and calmed your mind. It is such a great feeling to realize that you are getting better at thinking optimistically.

Some other tactics that you can use to learn optimism include:

1. Acknowledging That You Are Responsible For Your Perceptions

When negative things happen, it is easy for us to blame everyone else apart from ourselves. We blame others instead of sitting back and calling bullshit on ourselves. Acknowledging your role is the first step to becoming more optimistic and opening yourself up to new possibilities. Failure to do so can result in you becoming a victim of everything happening around you. Your perception of your life directly shapes your reality. Every living person has their definition of life, which extensively influences their destiny.

2. Considering That There Are Other Ways of Looking at Things

You may achieve this by shifting your perspective from negative thinkers to a positive one by consciously thinking happy thoughts. Experts refer to this tactic of learning optimism as "positive reframing." It involves challenging yourself not to look at the negative side of things, even though they may be glaringly obvious. But instead, focus on the positives and what you can gain or what lessons can be learned.

3. Being Careful of the Company You Keep

Learning to be optimistic will prove very difficult if you keep friends who are major gossipers or complainers. Keep that negative bullshit away from you, because negativity is contagious. In this scenario, it's only a matter of time before you join the bandwagon of Debbie Downers and Negative Nathans. The good news, however, is that positivity is also contagious. Let go of the wrong company and start connecting with optimistic people. You'll soon benefit from their positive energy instead and start to live a positive life.

4. Turning off the News

These days it's rare to turn on the news, read the papers, or read any online news without getting overwhelmed with negativity and taking on a gloomy outlook of the world. Let's face it; the news is depressing as hell. The fact is that you see an imbalanced view of the world. There are lots of good things happening around the world as well, but they seldom make the news. The media loves to report the negative shit, instead of focusing on how we can solve the issues or what is being done to solve them. For your good, turn off the news or watch only a limited amount. Instead, spend your time participating in activities that can help maintain your health and create a positive outlook.

5. Writing in a Journal for a Few Minutes Each Day

Learning optimism is not complete until you develop a habit of showing gratitude for the things that are valuable and meaningful to you. Start a journal and spend a few minutes each day writing down all the things for which you're grateful. By being appreciative and reflecting on the positives at the end of each day, you will train your mind to foster an optimistic outlook.

Chapter 2: **Becoming a Daily Optimist**

Some people are naturally optimistic, whether due to their genetics, environment, or upbringing, while others must learn how to be optimistic.

Either way, optimism is not a fixed characteristic, but a choice that we all have control over.

A once-optimistic person can become pessimistic, and a once-pessimistic person can also become an optimist. It is up to you to make yourself happy and consciously maintain a positive outlook regardless of your current situation. But how do you stay positive when faced with dire circumstances?

Having explained some of the many benefits associated with optimism, hopefully, you feel motivated to take the bold step to practice the habit of becoming a daily optimist. After you have made that decision, your brain will gradually become attuned to your new way of thinking and will adapt to it. Eventually, your brain will open new neural pathways or regular patterns of contentment, emotional stability, positivity, competence, joy, and getting out your own way.

As your intention to become a daily optimist strengthens, you will begin to see problems and challenges as stepping-stones instead of roadblocks. Rather than walking away when you encounter a challenge, you will plan a course of action, seek the advice of experienced and qualified individuals, and remain focused on a positive solution.

Becoming a daily optimist is life-changing. Once you begin, you will begin to see the results and enjoy its benefits almost immediately. So, stay the course and maintain a positive outlook even when the situations around you seem otherwise.

Before long, you will be overjoyed in the excitement of your determination to become a daily optimist as you see your hard work paying off.

We can all develop the necessary skills to improve optimism whether we are born with it or not.

Below are some practical tips on how you can invite optimism into your daily life.

Find the Opportunity in Every Difficulty

An optimist always focuses on the positives of every situation. They see opportunity where others see uncertainty and despair. For example, when I lost vision in my left eye, from a car wreck, I said to myself "I still have vision in my right eye and I am still alive." Note, however, that becoming a daily optimist does not mean ignoring problems. It means acknowledging that setbacks are inevitable but temporary and that you have all it takes to move past the current challenges and into a brighter future.

Allow Yourself to Experience Disappointment

One of the best skills you can learn while becoming a daily optimist is allowing yourself to experience disappointment. What this means is that you should not misunderstand optimism as simply looking on the bright side. Appreciate that nothing in life is permanent – however good or bad a situation is now; it will inevitably change.

The most important thing is to live in the moment when you're passing through those difficult circumstances. Take some time to envision the future and focus on the hope that the situation will improve.

Spend Time with Positive People

Your social circle plays an important role in your future success and can greatly impact your ability to think positively as well. There are certain behavioral patterns and emotions people project that you need to avoid. If someone is constantly negative, their negativity may rub off on you and ultimately drain the hell out of your spirit. Stay away from such people or develop strategies to help you limit your exposure to them. Instead, surround yourself with people who will lift your spirit.

Be Realistic, and Expect Ups and Downs

Save yourself from unnecessary disappointment by bringing yourself to the realization that nothing is perfect. Being an optimist doesn't mean you're immune to experiencing bad days. You cannot entirely avoid bad days. Life isn't a bed of roses; sometimes you may get caught up in a wave of troubles you never expected. Recognizing that these ups and downs are all part of being alive will help you let go and be at peace with the way things are.

Work Only on the Things You Can Control

One of the negative consequences of pessimism is that it breeds indecision. When you keep worrying about something that hasn't even happened yet, it prevents you from getting things done now. You end up wasting your time and losing out on enjoying what life has to offer. To avoid falling into this trap, acknowledge the things that you have no control over and don't become a victim. Refrain from thinking about what is happening to you, begin to strategize ways to fix the situation, and be gracious enough to accept the things that you cannot change. For example, you cannot control other people. I repeat you cannot control other people's thoughts or actions. Stop trying because the shit will not work. People will do and say what they want when they want.

Focus on the Present

Most people are too obsessed with their past and worry too much about their future while failing to see what's in the present. You need to understand that it will be difficult for you to appreciate the good things happening now if you lose your mind at another time. Accept your past, manage the present and work hard towards the future. More importantly, take control of your mind and concentrate on living in the present moment; you will be better for it. The past is behind you and you are not going backwards. Learn the lessons and move forward with your life.

Give Love, Receive Love, and Invest in Love

As they say, love makes the world go 'round – it is the greatest force in the universe. Many people would give anything to experience love, yet it doesn't cost anything for you to give or receive it. Love is immensely abundant, and you can extend it to anyone you meet – friends, family, co-workers, and even strangers you've only just met. It feels wonderful to practice random acts of kindness. Love is a great boost for positivity and acts as a protective shield against negativity – it heals, inspires, forgives, and encourages. So, share love wherever and whenever you can. Invest in it every day, for it means investing in your life.

Try to See the Bigger Picture

Pessimists usually fail to see the bigger picture when faced with a particularly challenging situation. They instead fall victim to what is known as 'the recency effect.' It's a psychological term used to describe the instance when we allow very recent experiences to affect our decision-making, due to the belief that those experiences are likely to continue indefinitely. Pessimists are often victims of the recency effect. Unlike optimists, they are quickly put off by the slightest challenge they face. They only plan short-term and are ignorant of the possibility that things will eventually get better. Get your ass up and stop playing the victim. Get out of your own way and get your mind right!!

Dedicate Time Each Day to Strengthening your Parasympathetic Nervous System

Strengthening your parasympathetic nervous system means engaging in activities that aid in relaxation and a feel-good state. There are certain practices that you can engage in daily that will take you into a relaxed state, thereby increasing your optimism. Some of these practices include meditation, yoga, and journaling. Some other effective activities include watching a funny movie, playing with kids or pets, listening to music, dancing, and singing.

Count your Blessings

One of the simplest, most productive ways to become a daily optimist is to be appreciative of the good things in your life. Find some spare time in your busy schedule each day to pause and reflect on all the things that you are grateful for, no matter how small. Be thankful for everything you have, who you are, the people around you, and so on. Counting your blessings is a very effective way to boost your positivity and will help you sustain an optimistic attitude.

Disconnect for a Bit

In today's society, we get bombarded with too much information and a 24-hour news cycle of all that is going wrong in the world. When you allow too much of this negative news to flood your mind, it can adversely affect your outlook on life. You don't need to stay informed about every current event happening around the world. Not only does the news affect you, but social media also plays a large part in our world, our minds, and our confidence. We are so fixated on what others are doing, what they have, and what they look like, that we abandon our own lives. An easy way for you to combat this issue and increase your positivity is to disconnect. Log out of all your social media sites including virtual networks, turn off the TV, and focus on engaging in real-life activities.

Minimize (and Ultimately Discard) Negative Language from your Vocabulary

Before you can indeed become a daily optimist, you need to purge yourself of all kinds of negative language that you've been using. Replacing this negative language with a positive and inspiring one will significantly improve your natural optimism. Practice reframing your self-talk and what you say to others when challenges arise.

Chapter 3: **How to Get Your Mind Right Daily Guide**

Now that you have learned what optimism is all about and what you need to do to invite it into your life, it is now time for you to take some practical steps to make it happen. Below is an example of how you can invite optimism into your daily life. It also includes tips on how to make developing the practice more straightforward and more useful at the same time.

Monday

For most of us, Monday is the first day of the workweek. As we prepare for the day ahead, a familiar sense of gloom can take over us. Mondays are supposed to represent a fresh start to a week full of potential, but all too often, we lack the passion and motivation to pick ourselves up on a Monday morning. Does this sound like your typical kind of Monday? Well, pessimists typically feel this way, even those in fulfilling jobs.

The truth of the matter is that this feeling or the lack of optimism we frequently experience on Mondays is all about how our mindsets are programmed. According to Martin Boroson, the author of The One Moment Master, "We make Mondays so much more miserable by believing we should be more productive."

The Monday Blues, as we often call these feelings, are so prevalent that it has become a cultural experience. Many of us dread returning to our daily routine of commuting to work and then facing the mountain of tasks waiting for us at our desks. The weekend is over and it's time to return to our miserable ass jobs. The secret to avoiding the Monday Blues is inviting optimism into your life is by changing your mindset. Remember that every challenge you're currently dealing with on this particular day is all part of your growth process.

You can begin by seeing Mondays as the perfect day to do things that will make the rest of your week more productive and less chaotic. You can also change your mindset about Mondays by doing things differently on that day. For example, you can have something different for breakfast or drink a glass of warm water to aid your digestion throughout the day.

Tuesday

Tuesdays will often be a day filled with lots of activities, but it's also a day that provides you with an opportunity to reclaim the rest of your week.

That is especially true if you had an unproductive Monday. According to a survey carried out by Workopolis, we regard Tuesdays as the most productive day of the week.

By Tuesday, some of the working population have become immersed in their daily work routine. However, if by then you're among the people yet to get their groove back, you can try these tips:

- Go to bed early on Monday so that you can get up first thing on Tuesday.

- Get some exercise.

- Eat a healthy breakfast.

- Pick up something you intended to complete on Monday and finish it.

- Say no to things that hurt your productivity.

Wednesday

Getting through Wednesdays is a struggle for many, statistics describes Wednesdays as the most depressing day of the week. A day that our mood reaches its lowest point. Wednesdays fall right in the middle of the week, and it's a day where we feel the furthest away from the weekend. The weekend that has just passed as well as from the one coming up. It's easy to feel overwhelmed with work by this point in the week. It seems as though the next weekend will never arrive.

To invite optimism into your life on a Wednesday, you can start by saving the tasks that you most enjoy doing for those days. Remember that the week is not yet over so don't overwork yourself, but instead, save your energy for more important decisions and tasks. Avoid spending all of your energy on minor or irrelevant tasks and decisions that will deplete your thinking capacity.

Embrace the challenges that Wednesday's a.k.a Hump Day brings with them and see them as an opportunity for you to show the world your true substance. Leverage the obstacles that you encounter and use them as motivation for your success. The middle of the week certainly has its challenges, but you must face them head-on with the right attitude.

Also, focus on staying in the moment as much as possible. It is all too easy for our minds to drift towards the weekend while still stuck in the middle of the week. But thinking about the future and wishing it was already here is the perfect breeding ground for pessimism. By remaining focused, setting strict timeframes for each task, and avoiding procrastination, you will be able to get things done on Wednesdays without sacrificing your positive attitude.

Thursday

Thursday is the day where you try to complete the bulk of your work before Friday. If you want to have your Fridays to be less work-filled, you will need to ensure that you get all your pending jobs done by Thursday, and that is what can make this day dreadful for the pessimist.

Some ways in which you can invite optimism into your Thursdays are by scheduling intentionally.

That involves planning meetings and phone calls for days earlier in the week so that you have the time to complete vital tasks before the weekend.

Another way is by constantly evaluating your priorities to make sure you are concentrating your energy on the right activities. Once you've determined your priorities, focus on those tasks.

Doing this can eliminate one of the reasons people find Mondays so daunting—they tend to carry over too many important tasks until the next weekday, which loads them up with work, causing more stress.

Successful people tune out distractions, especially on Thursdays. They make the best use of every available minute so that they can get their work done before the end of the day on Friday. They find a quiet spot where they can work and keep distractions at bay. They also find shortcuts by seeking creative ways to produce top-notch results while saving time in the process. For example, you can create a template or an automated response that you can send out whenever needed so that you won't have to draft the same message over and over again.

Friday

How you end the workweek can significantly influence your productivity next week and may determine how relaxed you are over the weekend. As the last day of the workweek, people frequently think of Fridays as somewhat low-key days. A day where you're either tackling bigger projects or setting yourself up for success in the coming week.

We all want to have that Friday where we get the chance to work on a personal project, leave the office earlier than usual, or have an after-work celebration with our friends. Many view Fridays as one of the best days of the week because they see them as less structured, so they are at liberty to decide how they spend their time. Many even consider this day as an extension of their weekend.

On Fridays, everyone is thinking about the weekend and is eager to get home. As a result, productivity drops. Rather than just waiting for the workweek to end, you can do a lot on Fridays to make your Mondays more bearable. For example, you can have a little "handover" ritual, something like what you do when you're planning on going on a holiday. Prepare a to-do list and write down all the tasks that you need to complete on Monday.

On your to-do list, itemize the five things that you did well during the past week. After that, list two things that you plan to do differently in the coming week. By outlining your weekly activities on Fridays, you will feel a sense of accomplishment, while keeping in mind that you are growing and learning by contemplating what could have gone better during the week. Knowing that your Monday is planned out will also enable you to be relaxed and fully enjoy your weekend.

Saturday

The long-awaited weekend is finally here, and you can't wait to enjoy what it has to offer. People see Saturdays as less-structured days where they can decide how they want to spend their time.

However, just like every other day, Saturdays need planning as well. In today's world filled with so many distractions, if you don't have a plan for your Saturday, it can be easy to succumb to the "I'm tired" excuse which likely keeps you locked in the house.

Without a weekend plan, you may end up spending all your Saturday mindlessly watching television or browsing the internet. That can impair your positive mood and leave you feeling exhausted, even when you're not doing anything. However, you can boost your optimism on a Saturday by planning your activities for the day.

Psychology research reveals that we're often happier when we are anticipating an event.

Some of the activities you can do on a Saturday include maximizing your morning by getting up before your family and engaging in some personal pursuits or hobbies. You can also create traditions like making pancakes in the morning or scheduling nap time with the family in the mid to late afternoon, delegating your chores, and even cutting back on technology. These activities are good for your brain and in contrast to your usual workweek. By planning fun into your Saturday, you are much less likely to start another week wishing you'd had accomplished more or spent time with loved ones.

Sunday

Many people feel less optimistic about Sundays, mainly because it is the last day of their beloved weekend and the day before they begin their busy work week routine. Take the opportunity to enjoy some time away from anything that has to do with your work or business on Sundays. By engaging in activities that you enjoy, you will be more productive, refreshed, and ready to face the challenges of the coming work week.

Try spending some time alone on Sundays. That gives you time to reflect, clear your head, improve your creativity, and do the things you love to do.

You can pursue a passion, get some exercise, socialize, or spend time with your family.

You can also try doing something fun on Sunday nights so that you can enjoy a vibrant and productive Monday morning. Some activities you might engage in on Sunday evenings to help clear the Monday blues include; having a big dinner party with your extended family, volunteering at a favorite charity, or taking an early evening yoga class. Remember to get to bed early on Sundays too. Being sleep deprived as you start your week can quickly lead to pessimistic thinking.

Conclusion

Optimism is like the fuel that drives us to succeed when we are going through difficult times. You can define it as the tendency to believe, expect, or hope that things will ultimately turn out for the best. There are several benefits obtained from optimism including, superior health, greater achievement, and better performance, overall well-being, healthy aging, and better luck in love and relationships.

Some people are born optimists while others must learn it. We can practice optimism by simply and consciously changing our thought processes.

According to psychologist Charles Carver, we can also learn optimists through Cognitive Behavioral Therapy (CBT) which employs a technique where you begin to understand and challenge the cognitive distortions that you have about yourself, the world, and the future.

To fully invite optimism into your life, you need to take practical steps such as:

- Finding the opportunity in every difficulty

- Allowing yourself to experience disappointment

- Spending time with positive people

- Being realistic by expecting both ups and downs in life

- Working on the things that you can control

- Focusing on the present

- Changing your self-talk

By also following a weekly calendar of activities that can help you increase your optimism, you are sure to reap benefits for yourself and those around you.

The
Workbook

Opening Pep Talk

Why is Optimism Important?

Optimism plays a vital role in our ability to lead a happy and successful life. If you constantly find yourself with self-defeating thoughts in your mind, you will most likely become a victim of such thinking in the future. If, however, you focus your mind on positive things, you will most certainly attract all such positivity into your life.

By consciously developing an optimistic outlook on things and promoting only positive thoughts in your mind, you will enjoy the many benefits that come along with it.

Can Optimism Be Learned?

The good news about optimism is that it is a skill that can be taught and learned. Research shows that there are various strategies that we can use to learn optimism.

Being optimistic is a skill that can be simple to learn but requires consistent effort and practice. There are several ways to learn optimism, and one such way is through the ABCDE model proposed by psychologist Martin Seligman. The ABCDE represents Adversity, Belief, Consequence, Disputation, and Energization. These are the phases you need to go through for each problem.

Optimism is ultimately more about resilience than temperament. Most people have experienced difficulties and failures in their lives. It's the reaction to these adverse situations and what people tell themselves in their subconscious minds that matter.

Differences between Pessimists and Optimists

Pessimists can learn to be optimistic about failures by analyzing their reactions to adversity and handling things differently. An optimist might look on failure as an unlucky situation (therefore not personal), only a setback (not a permanent issue), and just one failure in one of many goals (therefore not pervasive).

So, we can see differences between pessimists and optimists and how they explain events to themselves in either a positive or negative way.

To explain this a bit further, look at three primary differences between pessimists and optimists:

Personalization:

Optimists believe events occur due to causes outside of themselves. Pessimists blame themselves for problems. So, optimists internalize positive events, and pessimists externalize them.

Permanence:

Optimists see issues as temporary and good things happen for permanent reasons. Pessimists see problems as permanent and good events are only temporary.

Pervasiveness:

A pessimist assumes failure in one area will replicate through their life. An optimist would take a positive outcome and use that to brighten the rest of their lives.

ACBDE Model by Martin Seligman[1]

A. Adversity:

When someone dashes past you, bumps into you and knocks your drink to the ground.

B. Belief:

You tell yourself (and believe), "That person deliberately bumped me and didn't even apologize, they got me fucked up!!

C. Consequence:

Feelings of bitterness and anger gradually overwhelm you and continue to be with you for the rest of the day.

D. Disputation:

You realize that the negative feelings you are experiencing will not yield any good for you and you decide to take a stand against it. You place yourself in the other person's shoes and begin to find reasons for their action. Perhaps they needed to rush to the emergency room or rush off to another pertinent crisis. You allow yourself to forgive, forget, and move on.

E. Energization:

Upon overcoming the negative feelings you once experienced, you feel energized and happy to have successfully taken control of your thoughts and calmed your mind. It is such a dope feeling to realize that you are getting better at thinking optimistically.

In an optimist's eyes the adverse event would be explained like this:

Personalization: External

I was going about my business, and someone bumped <u>into me.</u>

Permanence: Temporary

It was just a one-time occurrence, unlikely to happen again, and no lasting effects.

Pervasiveness: Specific

The problem was due to that specific person bumping into me. Not everyone bumps into me.

A pessimist would explain the same event like this:

Personalization: Internal

I was in the wrong place and wasn't watching what I was doing.

Permanence: Permanent

I'm clumsy, and I'm always bumping into people.

Pervasiveness: Global

I'm like that with everything I do. I'll never manage to be good at anything.

So, the path to learned optimism is to learn to consider alternative reasons for the adverse event and chose one that has the least **Permanency** (i.e., temporary) and least **Pervasiveness** (i.e., specific).

Self-Exercises

In this exercise, we're going to help you recognize **A**dverse experiences that happen to you and reasons with yourself about your **B**eliefs. You will investigate the **C**onsequences of the pessimistic beliefs and then bring into question your pessimistic beliefs by **D**isputing them. Having done that successfully, you will feel more **E**nergized and optimistic and better able to overcome adversity.

What you need to do is complete the following five debate sheets over the next two or three weeks. Note that the Adversity can be brought about through negative thoughts about a positive event. For example, you might have a promotion at work – a positive event. But, it brings about Adversity because you're worried that you cannot do the job.

So, you must write down the event that causes the Adversity. Ask yourself about your Beliefs and what the evidence is for those beliefs. Think about the Consequences of your pessimistic beliefs, what it means, what's the outcome likely to be. Then you must Dispute the beliefs. You must argue with yourself. It may help you to step outside of your involvement at a personal level and think of someone telling you about their beliefs. Can you tell them why they are wrong and why their beliefs are wrong? Ask a friend what they think if you're stuck for ideas.

Yes, I know, it's a lot to do, and it's not easy, but it is the key to successfully using the **ABCDE** technique and turning you from a pessimist into an optimist.

Example: **Debate Record – Positive Event**

Debate Record	Date: June 30, 2020	Time: 15:22
Adversity	I wrote an article on my blog, and it was picked up by the press. That resulted in loads of hits to my website. Now the organizers of a huge international summit have asked me to give a presentation. Nearly 1000 attendees will be there.	
Belief	I'm not good enough to give a presentation; I don't know enough about the subject. I've never given a talk in front of an audience before. I'm going to be completely out of my depth, will get a terrible response and the organizers probably won't pay me. I wish they hadn't asked me to talk and I wish I'd not written the article.	
Consequence	I'll have sleepless nights about this. The press will pick up on my dreadful presentation and I'll be the laughing stock. If I say I'm not going to accept the request, the organizers will think I'm a fraud and don't know what I'm talking about.	
Disputation	But hold on. I must be pretty good, or they wouldn't have asked me. Thousands of people talk in front of audiences without any problem. I do know my subject well; I've been learning about it for years and have written a very successful book. It will be a great promotion for me & could be the making of me.	
Energization	I can do this. I am now feeling relaxed about it and know that I'm more than capable. I can use the book I've already written as a guide for the presentation. This will give me a wonderful opportunity to expand my business.	

Example: **Debate Record – Negative Event**

Debate Record	Date: June 30, 2020	Time: 15:22
Adversity	I wrote an article on my blog and quite a lot of people commented on it saying that I was wrong and my writing was poor.	
Belief	They are right. I don't know my subject very well. I failed English at school so there's no way I should be writing blog posts. In fact, the whole website is poor.	
Consequence	I've lost all my enthusiasm now. I'll close down the site. It was going to be a site I earned money from, but I'll have to go and get a job now.	
Disputation	But this was just one post I made. I've posted dozens of articles over the past year, and people have always commented about how good they were and how much they learned from me. Besides, it's good to cause some controversy from time to time. It makes people react and take note. Anyway, it wasn't badlywritten.	
Energization	This should make my blog even more popular, why on earth should I want to stop now. The controversy is good and I should write more articles where people question whether I'm right. That could open up a real debate and bring in a lot more readers and potentially money.	

Debate Record 1

Debate Record	Date:	Time:
Adversity		
Belief		
Consequence		
Disputation		
Energization		

Debate Record 2

Debate Record	Date:	Time:

Adversity

Belief

Consequence

Disputation

Energization

Debate Record 3

Debate Record	Date:	Time:
Adversity		
Belief		
Consequence		
Disputation		
Energization		

Debate Record 4

Debate Record	Date:	Time:
Adversity		
Belief		
Consequence		
Disputation		
Energization		

Debate Record 5

Debate Record	Date:	Time:
Adversity		
Belief		
Consequence		
Disputation		
Energization		

Debate Record 6

Debate Record	Date:	Time:
Adversity		
Belief		
Consequence		
Disputation		
Energization		

Debate Record 7

Debate Record	Date:	Time:
Adversity		
Belief		
Consequence		
Disputation		
Energization		

Debate Record 8

Debate Record	Date:	Time:
Adversity		
Belief		
Consequence		
Disputation		
Energization		

Debate Record 9

Debate Record	Date:	Time:

Adversity

Belief

Consequence

Disputation

Energization

Debate Record 10

Debate Record	Date:	Time:

Adversity

Belief

Consequence

Disputation

Energization

Wrap-Up

Learning to be an optimist is simple, but not easy. It takes daily practice. However, the good news is that it's possible and you can turn yourself into the optimist you always wanted to be.

If you've followed this workbook, you will be able to start to lay really good foundations and start to look at the way you think and why you think that way and GET OUT OF YOUR OWN WAY! Make sure every time you feel negative about anything fill out one of these Debate Records. Don't rush the exercise, take your time, and properly debate with yourself about your beliefs.

If you feel that you need to ask someone else about issues, which will genuinely help. It will benefit you to see outside of your beliefs and bring an extra dimension to your thinking.

Within a short while, you'll begin to understand where your pessimistic thoughts originate from and turn them around. You'll see the many benefits of being an optimist, and why practicing a positive outlook on life is KEY to your well-being, relationships, and career.

To your success!

Shauntee B

Note Pages

_____

_____

_____

_____

_____

_____

_____

_____

_____

_____

_____

_____

_____

_____

_____

_____

_____

_____

_____

References

[1]Seligman, Martin. Learned Optimism. New York, NY: Pocket Books. 1998.

Discovery Health. *Learned Optimism Yields Health Benefits.* American Psychological Association, 1997. Learned Optimism Yield Health Benefits.

https://kovamag.com/explanatory-style/

References

About the Author

WHO IS SHAUNTEE B?

STAY FLY, BE FIT, and LIVE RICH! That's how Shauntee B. lives her life, and as a serial entrepreneur, her businesses reflect this.

Girl Get Your Closet Right, a posh women's boutique, is the brainchild of Atlanta businesswoman Shauntee B. Her lifelong love of fashion and shoes, along with a desire to empower other women, resulted in her creating the boutique.

Her mission began with her passion for empowering women. Her online empowering groups (including the popular "Girl, Get Your Mind, Body, & Business Right!), fitness challenges, affirmations, and events are all centered around the goal of helping women feel better about themselves, both inside and out. Shauntee B provides lifestyle essentials for your MIND, BODY, CLOSET, and BUSINESS.

Her products, resources, and tools are all chosen to enhance your lifestyle and empower you for success in all areas: mentally, physically, spiritually, and financially. And, of course, all while looking fly.

Early on, she had to learn that resilience required resistance. As a teenage mother, she survived an abusive marriage and began to forge a path ahead built on her own strength. Resisting all the negative influences in society, while making her own path to enrichment, has been Shauntee B's mission. She's taken on the great city of Atlanta by storm, hosting her signature event "A Night of Luxury," a dinner party that celebrates women's ("Her") Black excellence.

From the Boutiques Wholesale Program, Mobile Boutique Services, Accountability Movement, and her continuing mission to raise awareness that women can do anything.

It's all about the creed: STAY FLY, BE FIT, and LIVE RICH. It's all within your grasp as Shauntee B provides you with all the resources in one place. You deserve it, so why not join Shauntee B on the journey of a lifetime today.

www.ingramcontent.com/pod-product-compliance
Lightning Source LLC
Chambersburg PA
CBHW050540270326
41926CB00015B/3322